Table of Con

MW00805954

$8.95

Bark Rubbing Collage

Nature Connection:

The trunk of a tree carries nutrients to every part of the tree. It is protected by an outer skin called bark. Some barks are thick, some are thin. Some have deep ridges, some are smooth. When a tree grows, its bark splits and cracks. Have children capture a tree's unique character by making and decorating a bark rubbing.

What You Need:

- heavy drawing paper
- construction paper, 9" x 12", any color
- outdoor area with several kinds of trees
- crayons
- masking tape
- white glue
- scissors

What You Do:

1. Visit an area where there are several different kinds of trees.
2. Choose one tree, tape the heavy drawing paper over its bark, and rub with a crayon until an even impression is made.
3. Repeat this process with three or four different trees and separate sheets of paper.
4. After returning to the classroom, cut the bark rubbings into many different interesting shapes.
5. On a piece of construction paper, assemble and glue pieces from the different rubbings to make a Bark Rubbing Collage.
6. Display the collage on a wall.

Try This:

You may make rubbings of leaves or rocks using the same method, but will have better success with thin paper.

Dried Flower Pocket

Nature Connection:

Some blooms, like straw flowers, zinnias, lavender, and statice, dry better than others. Air drying is the most popular (and easiest) method of drying flowers. The best time to harvest flowers is on a sunny morning after the dew has evaporated. Pick the best, long-stemmed blossoms just as they open and when their colors are at their brightest. After drying, display flowers in this personalized holder.

What You Need:

- paper plate, 8" diameter
- magazine pictures, markers, paint, and/or crayons
- yarn *or* ribbon
- assortment of dried flowers and foliage
- white glue
- ruler
- stapler
- hole punch
- scissors

What You Do:

1. Dry a collection of summer flowers by tying them in bunches and hanging them upside down out of sunlight in a well-ventilated room. (This will require 4–10 days.) Set aside.
2. Use magazine pictures, markers, paint, and/or crayons to decorate the *bottom* of the paper plate. Cut the paper plate in half.
3. Put the plate halves together (decorated sides out) and anchor with a few staples around the round edges.
4. Punch holes around the round edges at 1" intervals.
5. Lace ribbon or yarn through the holes, leaving enough at the ends to tie together for hanging.
6. Fill the holder with dried flowers and hang.

Try This:

Cut a paper plate in half and decorate the bottom of one half. Roll the decorated section into a cone. Staple the top opposite sides and punch holes near each of these staples. Push one end of ribbon or yarn through one of these holes, thread through the second hole, and pull out. Tie the two ends together. Fill this cone-shaped holder with dried flowers and hang.

Homemade Fossil Prints

Nature Connection:

Fossil prints found today were formed many years ago. When a leaf or shell fell into the soft mud, it was covered up and eventually the mud hardened into rock. All that is left today is a print of the original leaf or shell in the rock. Modern day "fossil" prints are easy and fun to make.

What You Need:

- self-hardening clay
- tagboard strip, 1' x $\frac{1}{2}$"
- plant, twig, *or* shell
- wax paper
- stapler

What You Do:

1. Form the tagboard strip into a circle and hold the form with a staple. Set it on a work surface covered with wax paper.
2. Form a smooth ball of clay. Press it inside the tagboard circle, making sure the clay reaches the sides of the tagboard.
3. Place the plant, twig, or shell specimen on the clay and carefully press it into the clay to make an impression.
4. Carefully lift the specimen out of the clay.
5. Set the clay "fossil" aside and allow it to harden.
6. After the fossil is hard and dry, remove the tagboard circle from the fossil.

Try This:

The fossil print may be used as a paperweight or decorative display. To hang the fossil, press a large, sturdy paper clip into the clay before the clay dries and hardens.

Maraca Gourds

Nature Connection:

The gourd plant is a vegetable that produces the inedible gourd fruit. There are two common types of gourds grown in North America: the thin-skinned ornamental gourd and the hard-shelled bottle gourd. They are grown from seeds and have yellow or white blossoms. Gourds may be shaped into dippers, spoons, bowls, holiday decorations, drums, or rattles. Students may want to try their hands at turning this unusual vegetable into a musical instrument!

What You Need:

- bottle gourd
- bucket of water
- tempera or acrylic paint *or* permanent markers
- small paintbrush for each color of paint
- foam cup for each color of paint
- steel wool *or* sturdy potato brush
- work gloves
- drill (optional)
- paper towels (optional)
- microwave (optional)

What You Do:

1. Soak the gourd in water for 30 minutes.
2. Wearing work gloves, scrub the gourd with steel wool or a potato brush to remove dirt and mold.
3. Allow the gourd to dry thoroughly, until you can hear the seeds shaking inside. (To speed up the drying process, which may take several months naturally, drill a small hole in each end of the gourd, place it on absorbent paper towels, and microwave at 30% power for 15 minutes or until the moisture is gone.)
4. Use the permanent markers or paint to create colorful designs on the bulb of the dried gourd.
5. Hold a maraca concert!

Try This:

For a holiday decoration, stand the gourd on end and paint a scene (snowman, tree, black cat, etc.) on its best side. Display the festive vegetable during the holidays.

Nature Detective Kit

Nature Connection:

The study of living things is called *biology*. Biologists learn about plants and animals by making observations, forming ideas (theories), and doing experiments. As students use their Nature Detective Kit, have them learn to be good biologists by being as accurate as possible in their observations. Have them collect and label their specimens carefully and keep records of their experiments.

What You Need:

- detective patterns (page 7)
- information cards (pages 8–9)
- shoe box
- spray paint *or* adhesive-backed white paper
- colored pencils, crayons, markers, etc.
- colorful ribbon, string, *or* wide, strong rubber band

As many of the following as possible:
- disposable camera
- several small plastic bags
- tweezers
- magnifying glass
- several small jars (with lids)
- small wire-bound notebook
- pencils and crayons
- glue stick
- scissors
- 6" ruler

What You Do:

1. Spray paint the shoe box or cover it with adhesive-backed white paper.
2. Decorate the outside with colored pencils, crayons, markers, etc. Copy, color, and cut out the detective patterns to glue onto the shoe box, if desired.
3. Collect and pack as many of the suggested items as possible in the detective kit. Copy and cut apart the information cards and place them in the kit. Use the cards to record information while exploring.
4. Tie the ribbon or string around the box or use a strong rubber band to keep the items from falling out.
5. Collect, label, and record your observations of nature. Have fun!

Try This:

Instead of a shoe box, spray paint and decorate an old lunch box to use as a carrying case. A lunch box may be slightly more costly, but it is much more portable and convenient.

Nature Detective Kit

Fall

Nature Detective Kit

Bugs

_____

_____

_____

_____

_____

_____

_____

Birds

_____

_____

_____

_____

_____

_____

_____

Plants

Animals

Porcupine Pinecone

Nature Connection

A porcupine is a rodent with long, sharp bristles of hair, called *quills*, all over its body. It defends itself by striking attackers with its quilled tail. Porcupines can be seen in the branches of *coniferous* (cone-bearing) trees, eating the bark. Porcupines inhabit cone-bearing forests all over North America. Use a part of their habitat, a pinecone, to create this cute, decorative porcupine.

What You Need:

- large pinecone
- 2 medium-sized black buttons *or* wiggly eyes
- 1 small black button
- 4 black pompons, ½" diameter
- toothpicks
- white glue
- picture of real porcupine for reference

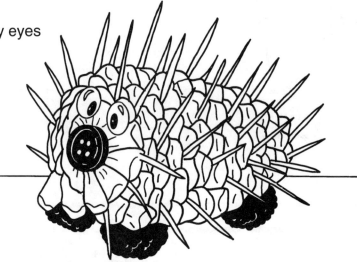

What You Do:

1. Glue two medium-sized buttons or wiggly eyes onto one end of the pinecone for eyes.
2. Glue the small button underneath the eyes for a nose.
3. Glue the pompons on the bottom of the pinecone to represent squatty feet. Let all materials dry completely.
4. Put a small dab of glue onto the end of a toothpick and push it into the pinecone. Hold the toothpick in place until it dries enough to support itself. Repeat this all over the pinecone, except for the underside.
5. When all materials are dry, display the porcupine pinecone on a shelf or desk.

Try This:

Make an edible porcupine by pushing small, straight pretzels into a large marshmallow, covering all but a "face" area. Use any number of edible treats, such as mini chocolate chips or dark candies, attached with a dab of peanut butter, for facial features.

Printed Place Mats

Nature Connection

Fruits and vegetables are an important part of a healthy diet. People eat the roots, leaves, flowers, and stems of most fruits and vegetables. Celebrate not only the importance of fruits and vegetables, but also the beautiful textures and designs that these foods can create, by making these colorful place mats.

What You Need:

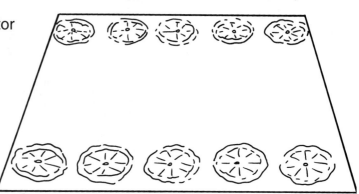

- light-colored construction paper *or* lightweight tagboard, 12" x 18"
- assorted fruits and vegetables, such as potatoes, apples, oranges, and carrots
- clear adhesive paper, 12" x 18" *or* a laminator
- thinned tempera paint, various colors
- foam cup for each color of paint
- 1" paintbrush for each color of paint
- scissors
- kitchen knife

What You Do:

1. Have an adult cut the vegetables and fruits in half. If desired, have the adult carve shapes into the flat surfaces with a kitchen knife. (The cut vegetables and fruit can be used like stamps for printing.)
2. Brush paint lightly on the cut sides of the vegetables and fruits.
3. Carefully press them onto the place mat to make an interesting design. Set aside to dry.
4. Use the scissors to round the corners of the place mat or to make decorative edges all around the place mat.
5. Cover with clear adhesive paper or laminate.
6. Use the new place mat to enjoy a snack of the fruits and vegetables (without paint!) that were chosen for this activity.

Try This:

If using real fruits and vegetables is not an option, glue pictures cut from a magazine onto the place mat for a nice collage.

Rainy Day Art

Nature Connection:

Rain forms when water droplets in clouds combine, become heavy, and fall to the earth. The effects of rain are numerous—from eroded soil to a washed-away chalk drawing. Take advantage of the next rainy day to create a colorful rain-splattered painting.

What You Need:

- watercolors *or* nonpermanent markers (any color)
- drawing paper
- paintbrush
- paper to cover ground
- rocks *or* paperweights
- rainy day

What You Do:

1. On a rainy day, paint a design of large colorful shapes on drawing paper. Do not allow the painting to dry completely.

2. Set the painting outside in an area where it will get wet but will not be blown away. Anchor the corners down with rocks or paperweights. If the art is placed on the ground, set it on another piece of paper first and then anchor the corners.

3. After a few minutes in the rain, bring the painting in and observe the various designs, shapes, and splotches that the rain drops created. Set aside to dry.

Try This:

Set similar paintings outside during different types of rain storms and compare and contrast them. How do similar paintings look after a light drizzle as opposed to a hard downpour?

Fall

Spider Web

Nature Connection:

Spiders all have eight legs, but only a few species of spiders live in webs. Web-spinning spiders emit a liquid silk from tubes (called *spinnerets*) in their abdomens. The liquid dries in the air and creates a web. Students can model a spider's web with common household items.

What You Need:

- spider pattern (page 14)
- bug patterns (page 14)
- cardboard circle *or* paper plate, 8" diameter
- gray *or* black yarn
- scissors
- adhesive tape
- hole punch

What You Do:

1. Make 1" cuts around the edge of the plate, approximately 2" apart.
2. Slip the end of the yarn into one of the slits and tape the end to the back of the plate.
3. Pull the yarn across the front of the plate and insert it into the slit that is on the opposite side of the plate as the first slit.
4. Then, moving underneath the plate, insert the yarn into the slit to the right.
5. Pull the yarn back across the plate and insert the yarn into the slit to the left of the original slit. Repeat this pattern until all the slits have been threaded and a spoke-wheel effect has been created.
6. Leave about 8" of yarn hanging from the end of the weaving and cut.
7. Copy, color, and cut out the spider pattern and attach it to the free end of the yarn with tape.
8. If desired, copy, color, and cut out the bug patterns and tape them onto the web.
9. Punch a hole in the top of the plate. Insert a length of yarn through the hole and tie off the yarn for hanging.

Try This:

Silver glitter will also make an attractive web design on the plate. Spread glue in a web design on the plate and then sprinkle glitter onto the glue. Gently shake off excess glitter into a trash can and allow the glue to dry.

Spider Web

Sunny Sunflowers

Nature Connection:

The sunflower head is made up of many tiny flowers clustered together. It is called a *composite* flower. The most common type of sunflower varies in size from three to ten feet tall. Sunflower seeds can be roasted and used as snacks, combined with other seeds for birdseed, or processed for cooking oil.

What You Need:

- petal patterns (page 16)
- leaf patterns (page 16)
- yellow tissue paper
- brown construction paper circle, 5" diameter
- small package of sunflower seeds *or* a black crayon
- green construction paper
- white glue
- scissors

What You Do:

1. Cut out the petal patterns and use them to trace and cut out 15–20 petals from the yellow tissue paper.
2. Glue the yellow petals in several layers around the edge of the brown paper circle. Allow to dry.
3. Glue sunflower seeds to the center of the flower. If seeds are not available, draw seeds with a crayon.
4. Cut two 1" strips of green paper. Glue them together to make a long stem.
5. Using the leaf patterns and green construction paper, cut out 4–5 leaves. Accordion-fold the stem so that it can be unfolded and give the impression of "growing." Glue the leaves to the back of the folded stem.
6. Display the sunflower on a door, window, or classroom wall.

Try This:

Make this sunflower into a sunflower person. Cut two additional 1" strips from green paper and fold to make arms. Attach the arms to the sunflower, then glue on wiggly eyes for a funny face.

Sunny Sunflowers

petal

leaf

petal

leaf

Wind Chimes

Nature Connection:

For centuries, people have managed to "harness" the wind to help them irrigate crops and create energy, for instance, with windmills. The wind has also been used to fly kites, push sailboats, and play wind chimes. Children can harness their own wind energy by making a wind chime that will clink and clatter in the breeze.

What You Need:

- long stick *or* dowel rod, 12" length
- 6–8 shells, large nuts, *or* small sticks
- string *or* thread
- thin cord
- white glue

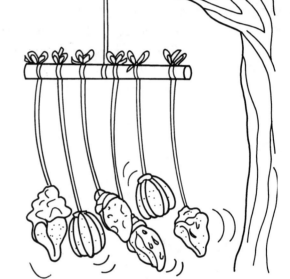

What You Do:

1. Tie several lengths of string to the long stick or dowel rod about 1¹/₂" apart.
2. Tie shells, nuts, or sticks onto the other ends of the string and secure with a drop of glue. Allow them to dry.
3. Tie the cord onto the middle of the stick or dowel. Be sure the weight is even on both sides of the cord so that it will hang evenly.
4. Hang the finished wind chime.

Try This:

Experiment using different materials to make wind chimes. What does a wind chime made with bamboo or wooden spools sound like? What does a wind chime made with rocks sound like?

Design-Your-Own Wreath

Nature Connection:

Because it is an unbroken circle, a wreath is thought to symbolize wholeness and continuity. Many wreaths are made of evergreen materials, symbolizing everlasting life. Children can make wreaths out of anything from pinecones to candy.

What You Need:

- bow patterns (page 19)
- wreath form cut from foam *or* cardboard, 8" diameter
- supply of small, clean twigs; pinecones; fruits; straw; waxy leaves; *or* dried berries, flowers, or plants
- cinnamon sticks *or* dried citrus slices (optional)
- ribbon, 1" width (optional)
- string, long enough to hang wreath
- spray paint (optional)
- white glue
- scissors

What You Do:

1. Spray paint the wreath form to give the wreath a colored background (optional). Allow to dry completely.
2. Glue the collected items onto the wreath form. Space larger items evenly around the wreath and then fill in the empty spaces with the smaller items.
3. Glue on a few sprigs of cinnamon or dried citrus slices, if desired, for fragrance.
4. Tie or glue a decorative ribbon bow to the wreath. If desired, use the bow patterns and simply color, cut out, and glue to the bottom of the wreath.
5. Tie the string to the top of the wreath for hanging.

Try This:

Try creating different shapes for wreaths. Traditional wreaths have a round, doughnut shape, but cardboard or foam can be cut into the shape of a heart, triangle, diamond, or square as well!

19

Winter

Lace Potpourri Sachet

Nature Connection:

Odors come from molecules of gas that have been released into the air. The nerves inside your nasal passages sense these molecules and send a message to the brain telling you that you smell something. Children can exercise their sense of smell by making this fragrant craft.

What You Need:

- dried flower petals, about ¼ cup (if more are needed, ask a florist for flowers that will be discarded)
- spices (such as cloves, cinnamon, and nutmeg), about 1 tablespoon of each
- lace *or* doily, 6" x 10"
- muslin, 6" x 10"
- potpourri oil (optional), available at craft stores
- ribbon
- small bowl
- spoon
- jar, bowl, *or* tin (optional)
- scissors

What You Do:

1. Lay the piece of lace on a flat surface, then place the piece of muslin directly on top of it. (The muslin will keep the potpourri from spilling out of the sachet.)
2. Mix the flower petals and spices together in a bowl. Add a few drops of potpourri oil, if desired, to intensify the scent.
3. Spoon a small mound of the potpourri mixture onto the center of the muslin.
4. Pull the corners of the lace and muslin up and tie the sachet closed with a ribbon.
5. Place any remaining potpourri in an open jar, bowl, or tin for others to enjoy.

Try This:

Many sweet-smelling plant materials can be combined to make this sachet. Use the finished sachet to freshen a drawer or to decorate a package or holiday table.

Living Terrarium

Nature Connection:

These small gardens, in closed or partially closed containers, can be used to grow a variety of plants and to learn about environments. With a little planning and care, children can simulate a natural environment that will last for a long time. A smaller terrarium can be created in a wide-mouthed jar or fish bowl.

What You Need:

- large, clear glass or plastic container
- removable lid *or* plastic wrap (for lid)
- several small plants
- charcoal, to fill 1" of container
- gravel, to fill 1" of container
- soil, to fill 1½" of container
- paper towel *or* cloth
- spoon
- sprayer filled with water

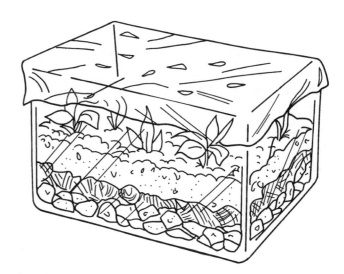

What You Do:

1. Spoon a 1" layer of gravel onto the bottom of the container.
2. Spoon a 1" layer of charcoal on top of the gravel.
3. Spoon a 1½" layer of soil on top of the charcoal.
4. Plant the plants so that no roots are exposed.
5. Moisten the soil with the sprayer. Wipe off the inside walls of the terrarium with a paper towel or cloth.
6. Place the cover on the terrarium so there is a small opening for air *or* cover the terrarium with plastic wrap and poke a few holes in the plastic with the end of the spoon.
7. Place the terrarium in light, but not direct, sun. Spray plants about once a week. If overwatering occurs and droplets can be seen on the side walls, leave the cover off for several hours until the excess water evaporates.

Try This:

Create a closed terrarium that shows the water cycle. Set a small container of water in your terrarium, then cover the opening of the terrarium with a glass pane or solid cover (a cookie sheet works well). Set the terrarium in a sunny location and watch the condensation collect on the underside of the cover and fall like rain.

Nature Collections

Nature Connection:

Children often enjoy trading items they have collected, such as trading cards, milk caps, small toys, etc. Allow children to gather natural items, such as shells or leaves, to create their own collections. Children may want to trade items before they place them permanently in their collection.

What You Need:

- variety of natural materials such as rocks, shells, seeds, pinecones, etc.
- egg carton *or* box lid and ruler
- small strips of paper
- fine line marker
- white glue
- reference books that identify specimens in the collection

What You Do:

1. Make sure all of the items are clean and dry.
2. If using a box lid, rule off an individual section in the lid for each item.
3. Glue each item in its lid area, *or* glue one item in each section of an egg carton. Allow to dry completely.
4. Look in reference books for the names of the specimens and label them accurately by writing the name of the specimen on a small strip of paper and gluing it below or beside the item.

Try This:

For show-and-tell or circle time, have the children present their collections. Ask the children to discuss the characteristics of their collections using describing words or answer these questions: Which item in the collection was the most difficult to find? What items in the collection are unusual? Which is your favorite?

Winter

Ornamental Pinecone

Nature Connection:

There are 550 species of conifer trees, the most common being fir and pine. The seed-bearing cones from these trees come in many shapes and sizes, and can make interesting decorations to display in the home.

What You Need:

- large pinecone
- loose, multicolored sequins and/or glitter
- string *or* gold cord (for wrapping packages)
- green tempera paint
- foam cup
- white glue
- 1" paintbrush
- scissors

What You Do:

1. Place a small amount of green paint in the foam cup.
2. Paint the individual tips of the cone green. Allow to dry completely.
3. Add small spots of glue on the painted cone and decorate it with sequins and/or glitter. Allow to dry completely. Gently shake the excess sequins and glitter into a trash can.
4. Wrap string or gold cord around the cone like tinsel.
5. Cut a length of string or gold cord and tie to the top of the cone for hanging.

Try This:

Hang the cone ornament outside on a tree branch to determine the humidity in the air. Moist air will cause the cone to open up while dry air will cause it to close. Remove the pinecone when the test is done so the decorations will not harm hungry birds or other animals.

Pot Sitters

Nature Connection:

Pot Sitters can be conversation starters and helpful ways to share information about plants. A tag attached to the Pot Sitter may instruct the reader about the species of plant or about proper plant care (i.e., "Needs direct sunlight."). The tag could also convey a special wish such as "Get Well!"

What You Need:

- tag patterns (page 25)
- small potted plant
- pompon, 1" diameter
- 3 pipe cleaners, 12" length
- craft stick
- wiggly eyes
- cardboard scrap
- scissors

- hole punch
- fine-point markers

What You Do:

1. Place a pompon in the center of a pipe cleaner and then fold the pipe cleaner in half, wrapping the pipe cleaner around the pompon. Twist the ends together to hold the pompon in place. Continue twisting the two ends together for about 2" to create a body. The remaining length will become legs. Bend the tips to make feet.

2. Place the middle of the second pipe cleaner at the point where the legs begin. Twist it up around the body, stopping just below the neck. The remaining length of pipe cleaner will become arms. Bend the tips to make hands.

3. Use the third pipe cleaner to secure the body to the top half of the craft stick. Cut off any excess pipe cleaner.

4. Glue wiggly eyes to the pompon head.

5. Bend the legs into a sitting position. Push the stick into the dirt at the edge of the pot. Let the knees of the Pot Sitter hang over the edge.

6. Cut a small piece of cardboard into a small tag (about $2^1/_2$" x $1^1/_2$"). Print a message on the tag or cut out and glue one of the tag patterns onto the cardboard.

7. Punch holes in each end of the tag. Insert the Pot Sitter's hands into the holes.

Try This:

Make several Pot Sitters to be houseplant markers. On the tags, write the names of plants, flowers, etc., to identify the potted plants in the house. Laminate the tags so they will last longer.

Pot Sitters

Use these pre-printed messages with the Pot Sitter.

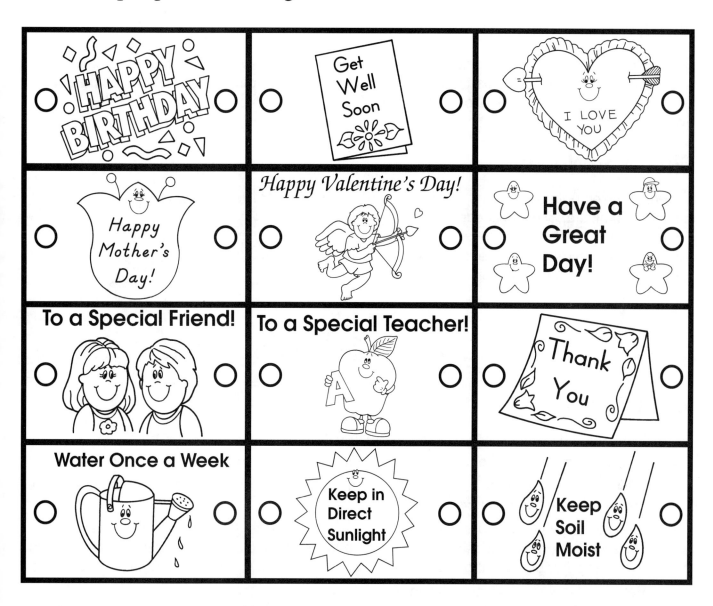

Or create your own messages.

25

Winter

Potato Creature

Nature Connection:

Besides grains, potatoes are the most important food crop in the world. The potato is actually a *tuber*, meaning the thickened part of the stem that grows underground. The flesh of the potato is *porous* (absorbent) enough to allow plant growth. Students can prove this fact by creating their own "hairy" potato creature.

What You Need:

- medium-sized potato
- rye grass, alfalfa, *or* cress seeds
- pieces of vegetables to make facial features (carrot "coin" eyes, red pepper slice mouth, etc.) *or* permanent, colored markers
- foam cup
- toothpicks
- paper towel

- sprayer filled with water
- spoon
- paring knife
- scissors

What You Do:

1. Have an adult cut about 1" from the top of the potato.
2. With a spoon, scoop about 1" of potato flesh from the top, leaving a rim around the edge.
3. Have an adult cut the bottom off of the foam cup. Turn the cup upside down and use it as a base for the potato creature.
4. Plan the facial features. Hold them in place with toothpicks. If you do not want the toothpicks to show, break them in half and push a halved toothpick into a vegetable piece. Then push the other end into the potato. (As an alternative, draw a face on the potato with markers.)
5. Sprinkle the seeds into the hole at the top of the potato. Mist the seeds well with water and cover them with a paper towel.
6. Keep the potato in a well lit area. Moisten the seeds 2–3 times per day until the seeds germinate (do not allow the potato to dry out). Remove the paper towel.
7. Allow the "hair" to grow tall. Trim as desired.

Try This:

Experiment by turning the potato sideways, planting different kinds of seeds, or adding pipe cleaner legs, wiggly eyes, or other items to decorate the "hairy" creature.

Teacup Garden

Nature Connection:

Some flowers grow from bulbs instead of seeds. *Bulbs* are made of overlapping leaves surrounding a young plant. We also use the term bulb to include *corms* (thickening stems with paper coats) and *tubers* (fleshy roots). All bulbs produce roots, leaves, and flowers. They store food and water and do not necessarily require soil to grow. Hardy bulbs will bloom only once indoors. Most bulbs flower best when planted in the fall and remain dormant until spring. Some common flowers that grow from bulbs include daffodils, tulips, crocuses, irises, and hyacinths. Students can fool (force) bulbs into blooming indoors during the winter by simulating desirable growing conditions.

What You Need:

- pretty teacup *or* small ceramic bowl
- 5–6 Dutch crocus bulbs
- potting soil
- water
- large spoon
- refrigerator *or* other cool, dark place

What You Do:

1. Spoon the potting soil into the container to about ½" from the top.
2. Place the crocus bulbs close together in the soil without touching, with their tips showing slightly (the flat part of the bulb is always the bottom).
3. Place the container in a refrigerator or other cool, dark place for 6–10 weeks.
4. Check about once a week to be sure the soil is moist. Do not overwater, but do not allow the soil to dry out completely.
5. When the crocuses begin to sprout, move them to a warm indoor spot in direct sunlight, possibly on a window sill. Flowers should open in about four weeks.

Try This:

Begin this project around the beginning of spring so the flowers will be blooming or ready to bloom for Mother's Day. Tie ribbon to the container to make the plant more decorative, or paint and decorate the container especially for Mom!

Winter Bird Feeder

Nature Connection:

Many birds live in one place during the summer and another place during the winter because of the availability of food. The birds' flight to follow a food supply is called *migration*. Some birds, however, do not leave cities in winter. Their nests are protected by buildings, and temperatures are several degrees higher than in the surrounding countryside. These birds must rely on people for food in order to survive the winter. Here is something students can do to help.

What You Need:

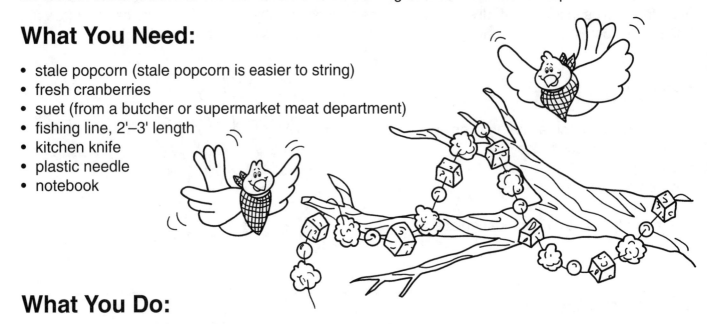

- stale popcorn (stale popcorn is easier to string)
- fresh cranberries
- suet (from a butcher or supermarket meat department)
- fishing line, 2'–3' length
- kitchen knife
- plastic needle
- notebook

What You Do:

1. Have an adult cut the suet into 1" chunks. Set the suet aside.
2. Put one end of the fishing line through the eye of the needle, pull a short length out, and tie a knot to secure the line onto the needle while stringing.
3. Make a large knot in the long, free end of the fishing line so that pieces will not fall off of it.
4. String the popcorn, cranberries, and suet pieces onto the fishing line.
5. Hang the finished feeder from the branches of a tree that can be seen from a window. Go inside and watch what happens.
6. Use the notebook to record how many birds come to the feeder and what color they are. See how long it takes for all the food on the feeder to be eaten.

Try This:

This project can reinforce patterning. Make a garland using a distinct pattern (i.e., two popcorn pieces, one cranberry, two pieces of suet, etc.) and then have a friend copy it. Try developing several different patterns.

Winter

Winter Seed-Storage Box

Nature Connection:

At the end of each growing season, most gardeners begin planning for the next year. Seeds can be collected and dried to be used the following season with minimum effort. Some seeds that can be saved are marigolds, snapdragons, zinnias, cosmos, and coneflowers. Students can share their seeds with other gardeners and expand their plant collections.

What You Need:

- flower/garden patterns (page 30)
- assorted seeds
- shoe box
- small envelopes (one for each type of seed)
- construction paper *or* white adhesive-backed paper
- pressed flowers (optional)
- pen *or* pencil
- scissors
- white glue
- crayons *or* markers

What You Do:

1. Write on the outside of each envelope the type of seed that will be placed inside, along with the growing and care instructions for the flower or plant. Place each type of seed in the correctly labeled envelope and seal.

2. Decorate a shoe box to create a bright, attractive storage container.
   (a) Cover the box with construction paper or white adhesive-backed paper. (b) Use crayons or markers to create flower or garden designs. Color and cut out the flower/garden patterns to glue onto the box, if desired. (c) Optional: Glue pressed flowers (preferably flowers for which you are storing seeds) on the box. (d) Print "Winter Seed Storage Box" on the lid.

3. Place the seed envelopes inside the box. Store your box in a safe place away from sunlight or moisture.

4. Plant the seeds the next growing season following the directions written on the envelope.

Try This:

Decorate the seed envelopes themselves to give as gifts. Place seeds inside the envelope and seal. On the front of the envelope, print the name of the flower or plant in large letters. Glue a pressed flower next to the name and cover the front of the envelope with clear adhesive-backed paper. On the back of the envelope, print the instructions for planting and growing.

Winter

Winter Seed-Storage Box

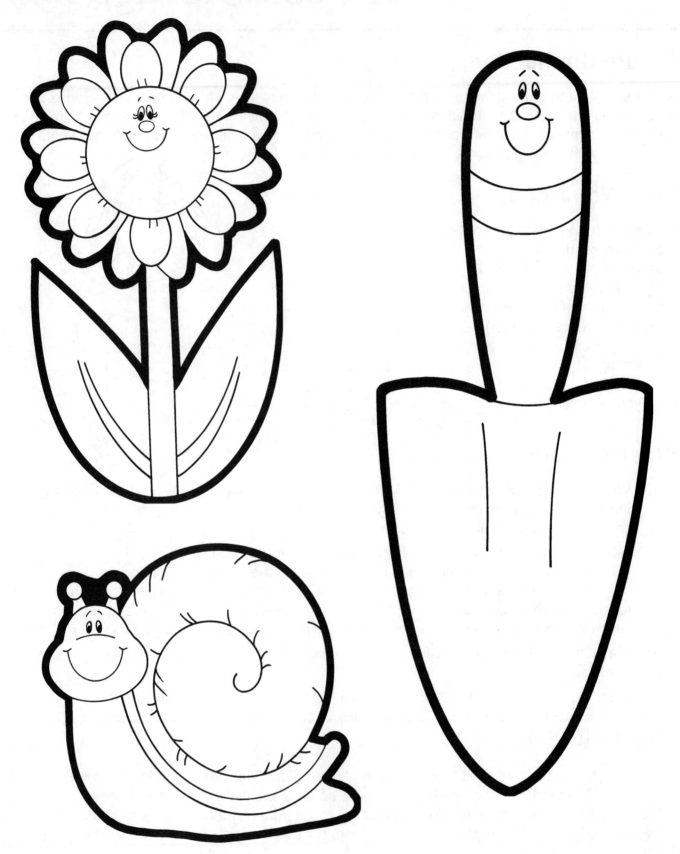

Bird-Nest Materials Box

Nature Connection:

While not all birds build nests in which to lay their eggs, the ones that do vary in skill and the materials they use. A swallow sometimes makes over 1,000 trips to collect all of its nest-building materials! It is easier for birds to build a safe home for their families if they can find the materials they need from a bird-nest materials box.

What You Need:

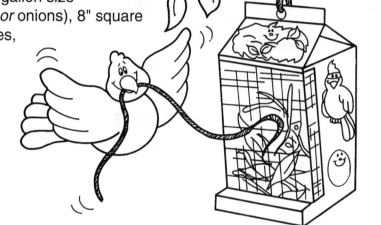

- decorative patterns (page 32)
- clean paper milk carton, gallon *or* ½ gallon size
- piece from mesh bag (from oranges *or* onions), 8" square
- bits of string, raffia, yarn, twigs, leaves, moss, and other nesting materials
- heavy string, 2' length
- white glue
- scissors
- craft knife
- hole punch
- gloves

What You Do:

1. Glue the top of the container closed. When it has dried completely, punch a hole in the top flap.
2. Insert heavy string through the hole and tie the string off for hanging.
3. Have an adult cut off one side of the milk carton, slanting down and slightly back at an angle. Leave the bottom of the carton fully intact. Birds can use the bottom flap to perch on.
4. Color and cut out the decorative patterns to glue onto the side of the box, if desired.
5. Fill the box with nesting materials. (Be sure to use gloves when collecting and handling these materials. Many birds will not use an item that has a human scent on it.)
6. Glue a piece of mesh across the exposed side.
7. Hang the nesting-materials box from a tree limb.
8. Watch the birds as they take materials from the box.

Try This:

Construct a second Bird-Nest Materials Box filled with different materials such as pine needles, straw, etc. Keep a record of the types of birds that choose materials from each box.

Bird-Nest Materials Box

Bug Keeper

Nature Connection:

Insects are six-legged animals that have three main body parts: head, thorax, and abdomen. It can be fascinating to observe an insect and its behavior. Children can make and use this economical Bug Keeper to temporarily house an insect.

What You Need:

- Bug Observations sheet (page 34)
- bug, such as grasshopper, ladybug, moth, etc.
- leaves and a twig
- water
- clean, dry, quart-sized milk carton
- old, light-colored nylon hose
- twist tie
- permanent marker
- ruler
- magnifying glass
- scissors *or* craft knife

What You Do:

1. Use the ruler to mark window openings on three sides of the carton. Leave a 1" margin on each side.
2. Have an adult cut out the holes.
3. Place the carton inside the nylon hose and pull the hose up so that the toe is at the bottom of the carton.
4. Place some leaves and a twig in the carton. Add a few drops of water.
5. Now the Bug Keeper is ready for its first inhabitant.
6. Pull the nylon hose up to the top of the carton and secure with a twist tie.
7. Use the magnifying glass to study the insect. Use the Bug Observations sheet, if desired, to help record observations.
8. When the activity is complete, release the bug where it was found.

Try This:

Instead of placing the box inside nylon hose, wrap the Bug Keeper with a long piece of mesh from a mesh bag. The mesh should have very small holes so the insect can not escape. Glue the mesh so that it is secured tightly around the box.

Bug Keeper

Name: _____

1. Draw a picture of your bug:

2. Insects have six legs, and spiders have eight legs. How many legs does your bug have?

   _____

3. Does your bug have antennae? _____

4. What color is your bug? _____

5. What is the name of the type of bug you have? (If you do not know, look it up in an

   encyclopedia or an insect reference book.) _____

6. If you put leaves and grass in the bug keeper, is your bug eating them? How much does

   your bug eat? _____

7. Does your bug have wings? Is it trying to fly? _____

8. How did you capture your bug? _____

   _____

9. What will you name your bug? _____

10. Now let your bug go. What happened? _____

Decorative Fabric Pot

Nature Connection:

Bedding plants like marigolds, impatiens, chrysanthemums, or petunias are hardy and will have long-lasting, colorful blooms. Children may choose to start seeds, herbs, or small house plants in pots they have decorated themselves.

What You Need:

- terra-cotta pot, 4" tall
- fabric (small print *or* gingham), 15" square
- ribbon, 24" length
- small herb, flowering plant, *or* seeds
- potting soil
- water
- fabric glue
- pinking shears (optional)
- paintbrush

What You Do:

1. If desired, cut around the fabric edge with pinking shears.
2. Lay the fabric print-side down on the work surface.
3. Paint fabric glue on the outside of the pot.
4. Set the pot in the center of the fabric. Press the fabric around the pot up to the rim. (The excess fabric should form a gathered decorative edge.) Set aside to dry completely.
5. Plant the plant or seeds in the pot according to package directions. Water lightly.
6. Tie a ribbon around the rim of the pot.
7. Set the pot on a sunny window sill or give as a gift.

> ## Try This:
>
> If the pots are made during a time when the flowers might not bloom, plant imitation flowers instead. Cut out colorful flowers from construction paper and glue them onto drinking straws. Place the straws into the soil in the pot.

Flower Press

Nature Connection:

Pressing flowers is one of the simplest ways to preserve their beauty. Dry the flowers as flat as possible in a natural position, because they will be too fragile to move once they are dried. Some common flowers ideal for pressing include pansies, violets, crocuses, daisies, cosmos, geraniums, rose buds, (single) zinnias, and impatiens. Children can easily press flowers themselves by using this homemade flower press.

What You Need:

- flower patterns (page 37)
- piece of cardboard, 20" x 12"
- piece of cardboard, 9" x 11"
- absorbent paper (paper towels *or* blotting paper)
- 2 pieces of ribbon, 1" x 3'
- flowers for pressing
- glitter
- brad fasteners (optional)
- ruler
- pencil

- white glue
- crayons
- markers

What You Do:

1. Fold the 20" x 12" piece of cardboard in half so that it is now 10" x 12". The folded piece should open like a book.

2. Measure 3" from the top and bottom of the cardboard and draw a pencil line on the outside, front and back. Close the cardboard "book." Glue the ribbon along the lines, leaving the ends free to tie the press closed. Allow to dry.

3. Decorate the press with flower patterns, crayons, markers, and glitter. Print your name on the front.

4. Insert the extra piece of cardboard in the center of the press.

5. Place a flower between two paper towels or pieces of blotting paper and insert it *under* the extra cardboard piece. Repeat for a second flower and insert it *on top* of the cardboard.

6. Tie the press closed. If desired, have an adult poke holes along the edge of the press with scissors and insert brad fasteners to hold it tightly closed.

7. Check the plants periodically. Some will dry in 3–4 days.

> ## Try This:
>
> The dried flowers can be glued to greeting cards, bookmarks, or stationery, or arranged in a purchased picture frame. Pressed flowers can even be glued to the front of the press!

Flower Press

Spring

Framed Nature Picture

Nature Connection:

An organized collection of mounted pressed flowers is called an *herbarium*. Children can display their own pressed flowers or a variety of other natural objects with this homemade picture frame.

What You Need:

- 2 pieces of cardboard, 8" x 9"
- small-print or plain wallpaper *or* wrapping paper scraps
- several natural items: seeds, pressed flowers, foliage, twigs, nuts, etc.
- white glue
- scissors
- tweezers

What You Do:

1. On one of the cardboard pieces, measure a 1" border on all sides. Have an adult cut out the middle section. The remaining 1" border is the frame.

2. Glue decorative paper to the frame and set aside to dry completely.

3. Measure and cut more decorative paper to fit the remaining 8" x 9" cardboard piece. This is the backer.

4. Glue paper to the cardboard backer. Allow to dry completely.

5. Using tweezers, center the natural items in an appealing arrangement on the decorated side of the cardboard backer.

6. Carefully, working with one at a time, lift and glue the items into place. Be careful not to place any items where the frame will be. Allow the items to dry completely.

7. Glue the frame on top of the completed backer. The picture will last longer if displayed out of direct sunlight.

Try This:

Use contrasting paper for the frame and backer piece so the frame will stand out more clearly from the picture.

Leaf Prints

Nature Connection:

The veins of a leaf carry food and water throughout the leaf. The veins also support the leaf and help it keep its shape while also giving the leaf a distinct texture that children can use for decorating.

What You Need:

- blank writing paper and envelopes
- assortment of small leaves
- floral scented cologne (optional)
- thinned tempera paint
- foam cups for each color of paint
- 1" paintbrush for each color of paint
- paper towels
- roller

What You Do:

1. Apply a light coat of paint to the veined side of a leaf.
2. Carefully press the leaf (paint-side down) onto the corner or border of the blank paper or envelope.
3. Cover the leaf with a paper towel and rub gently with the roller.
4. Carefully remove the paper towel and leaf. Allow to dry completely. Continue the process until all decorations are complete.
5. Add a drop of floral fragrance to the paper, if desired.

Try This:

Use stationery with leaf prints for personal letter writing or give as a gift. This method may also be used to make original pictures or decorate folders or book covers. Try using different objects to make the nature prints. Flowers or even fingers make interesting prints!

Spring

Miniature Trellis

Nature Connection:

There are many vining vegetables and flowering plants that require support while growing. A full-size version of this miniature trellis (minus the plastic tray, of course) can be made from larger branches, nailed or tied together, and installed in the garden to hold pea or bean vines or flowering plants like roses or sweet peas.

What You Need:

- 6–10 straight, dry sticks, 8" length
- bag of Spanish moss (optional)
- brightly colored tissue paper, 3" squares
- deep, clean, plastic tray (from a frozen dinner)
- soil, sand, *or* gravel (enough to fill the tray)
- decorative paper
- crayons
- markers
- wood glue
- scissors
- spoon

What You Do:

1. Experiment with different criss-crossing arrangements for the sticks. Be sure that the base of the trellis will fit inside the plastic tray. Glue the sticks together. Set aside to dry.

2. Cover the entire tray with appealing paper. Use the crayons and markers to decorate the tray as desired.

3. Use the spoon to fill the tray with soil, sand, or gravel.

4. Twist the tissue paper squares into "flowers" and glue them onto the trellis. Add a little Spanish moss, if desired.

5. Stand the trellis up in the tray and push the gravel or other materials around the base so that the trellis will stand straight.

Try This:

Fill the plastic tray with potting soil. Plant bean or pea seeds and add the trellis. As the plants begin to grow, loosely secure the vines to the trellis with twist ties.

Multicolored Vase

Nature Connection:

Cut flowers need water to stay fresh. The water in the vase travels up the flower stems to the leaves and petals. After receiving or picking flowers, cut the stems at a diagonal angle and place them in warm water to encourage the flower to take up the water. Some blooms will last up to a week. Be sure to watch the water level and add more when needed.

What You Need:

- empty, clean plastic bottle (a large-sized salad dressing or ketchup bottle will work best)
- scraps of multicolored tissue paper
- flowers for vase (a florist may be able to provide "less than fresh" flowers so each child may have at least one for her vase)
- thinned white glue
- 1" paintbrush

  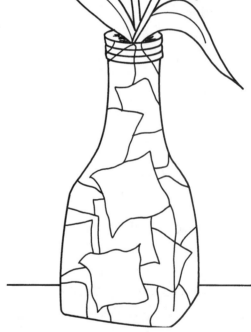

What You Do:

1. Paint glue on a small section of the bottle.
2. Lay the tissue paper pieces on the glue.
3. Continue until the bottle is covered. Allow to dry.
4. Paint a thin layer of thinned glue over the finished bottle and allow to dry completely.
5. Add another layer of glue for a final coat, then allow to dry again.

Try This:

After the final coat of glue is dry, glue an assortment of decorative items such as sequins, beads, stars, etc., to the outside of the vase. Put a flower in the vase and give it to a special person.

Nature Game

Nature Connection:

From the changes in a caterpillar's life cycle to the changes of the seasons, the wonders of nature are all around us. Discovering these wonders and learning about them can be great fun. Use this game to test students' knowledge of nature and help them discover new and exciting things.

What You Need:

- game rules (page 43)
- "How Does Your Garden Grow?" game board (page 44)
- game cards (page 45)
- acorns, small rocks, *or* other natural game pieces
- die
- file folder
- resealable, plastic sandwich bag
- scissors
- markers, various colors
- white glue
- laminator *or* clear contact paper

What You Do:

1. Duplicate a copy of the game rules, the game board, and the card patterns. Cut the cards apart. Use the blank cards for writing original questions, if desired.

2. Glue the game board and a copy of the rules to the inside of a file folder.

3. Have children write the title of the game on the outside of the file folder. They may use markers to decorate the outside of the folder as desired.

4. Laminate the completed game-board file folder and all cards for durability.

5. Glue a resealable, plastic bag to the back of the file folder. Store the cards, die, and game pieces in the bag.

6. Have children follow the rules to see who will win the game.

Try This:

To make the game last longer, a player must roll the exact number for the number of spaces to get to the finish line. If a nature unit is being taught, include possible test questions with the game cards so that students may study for the test while having fun!

How Does Your Garden Grow?

(for 2 or more players)

1. Each player chooses a natural game piece and places it on the START square.

2. Place the cards face-down on the CARDS space below.

3. Each player then rolls the die. The player with the highest number goes first.

4. The person to the player's right draws a card and reads the question to the player. The player must then try to answer the question (answers are printed upside down on the cards).

5. If the player is correct, he or she may roll the die and move his or her piece that number of spaces. The player must follow the directions on the new space, if there are any.

6. If the player is not correct, he or she remains in place and waits for the next turn. The card is placed face-down on the bottom of the stack. Play continues to the right.

7. The player to reach the FINISH square first wins!

CARDS

Spring

Nature Game

 **START**	The soil is just right for planting. Go ahead 1 space.		Sunny day! Everything is blooming. Go ahead 1 space.	
				Oh no! A late frost kills several plants. Go back 1 space.
	A gentle wind carries seeds for future plants. Go ahead 1 space.		Stung by a bee! Go back 1 space.	
An animal eats the vegetables you planted. Go back 1 space.				
	Aaaah! A refreshing rain helps everything grow. Go ahead 1 space.		Bees pollinate the flowers. Go ahead 1 space.	
				You see a rainbow. Go ahead 1 space.
 **FINISH**	A rainstorm washes away garden soil. Go back 1 space.		Baby birds are born. Go ahead 1 space.	

Spring

44

How many legs does an insect have? six (6)	Name three things most plants need to grow. water, light, and warmth (many need soil, too)	What does a caterpillar turn into? either a moth or a butterfly
What is the name of a bee's home? beehive	Is a reptile's blood warm or cold? cold	What is it called when an animal "sleeps" through winter? hibernation
Warm-blooded animals that have hair and give birth to live babies are called _____. mammals	How does a fish breathe? through gills	How many legs does a spider have? eight (8)
What covers and protects the bodies of snails, turtles, and crabs? shells	Turning old paper, plastic, or glass into new products is called _____. recycling	What covers most trees to protect them? bark
What is water that falls from clouds? rain	How many seasons do we have? four (4)	What covers a bird's body? feathers

Sponge-Spider Garden

Nature Connection:

Students usually think of plants only growing in soil, but some seeds will germinate and grow without soil. These types of seeds need only light and water. Students can prove this fact by "planting" seeds in a sponge and watching sprouts grow.

What You Need:

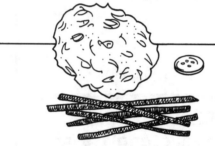

- piece of small natural sponge (available in the cosmetic section of most drug stores)
- rye, wheat, alfalfa, mung, *or* cress seeds
- small bowl
- 2 small buttons (with large holes)
- 5 pipe cleaners
- string, 36" length
- water
- spray bottle
- ruler

What You Do:

1. Tie the string around the sponge, leaving the ends free for hanging.

2. Insert one pipe cleaner through the top of one end of the sponge. Hang a button on each end of the pipe cleaner and curl the ends to hold them in place. These are the eyes. Trim off excess pipe cleaner.

3. Insert the other 4 pipe cleaners across the bottom of the sponge. Bend to make knees and feet. Arrange the legs as you wish.

4. Soak both sides of the sponge in a bowl of water and generously sprinkle the seeds onto the damp sponge.

5. Hang the sponge in a sunny window. Spray the sponge with water every day. Sprouts should appear in about 3 days.

6. Measure the sprouts daily to see how much they have grown.

Try This:

If hanging the Sponge-Spider Garden creature is not an option, set it on a window sill. If necessary, glue small pieces of cardboard on the bottom of the "feet" to help it "stand" better.

Toad Habitat

Nature Connection:

Toads are most active at night. They have long sticky tongues and strong legs for hopping. They are protected by thick, brown skin that makes them difficult to see in soil. Unlike frogs, toads live mainly on land. Toads are friends of gardeners because they eat harmful insects. Toads will enjoy the natural habitat of a garden, if they are provided with a safe home and a fresh water supply.

What You Need:

- 2 plastic bowls, at least 6" in diameter
- fist-sized rock
- leaves, bark, twigs, acorns, rocks, etc.
- water
- scissors
- white glue
- garden trowel

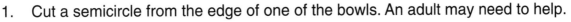

What You Do:

1. Cut a semicircle from the edge of one of the bowls. An adult may need to help.
2. Glue leaves, bark, acorns, etc., to the outside of the bowl as camouflage.
3. Choose a shady spot in your garden to create the habitat.

    (a) Loosen the dirt with the trowel.

    (b) Pour some water on the ground to make a soft mud.

    (c) Set the bowl upside down and press the bowl back down into the mud. Be sure to leave enough room inside the bowl for the toad!

4. Create a pool for the toad in the new habitat.

    (a) Dig a hole in the ground near the toad house to hold the other bowl.

    (b) Put the rock in the bowl.

    (c) Fill the bowl with water.

5. Camouflage the area with leaves, rocks, and twigs.

Try This:

Choose different sized bowls to attract different sized animals. Camouflage each "habitat," then check each day for new animals or insects.

Worm Farm

Nature Connection:

Worms make an important contribution to the garden by *aerating* (exposing to air) and fertilizing the soil as they tunnel through it. They like warm, moist soil with lots of organic matter to eat. After children have raised several worms, they should move a few into their garden where the worms can help improve the soil.

What You Need:

- plastic dish pan *or* a large box lined with a black plastic garbage bag
- garden soil
- peat moss
- a few fresh leaves
- 12 large worms (earthworms work best)
- water
- small spade

What You Do:

1. Fill the container ³/₄ full with soil. Add a 3" layer of peat moss on top of the soil. Moisten with water and allow to sit for a few days.

2. Mix the soil, leaves, and peat moss well with the spade and add the worms. These may be dug from a yard or purchased from a bait store.

3. Keep the soil moist and mix it gently with a spade every few days.

4. Add more soil and peat moss if needed.

5. Move some of the worms to the garden every month to help make the soil fertile. The worms will continue to reproduce as long as the farm is kept moist, the soil is turned periodically, and a few fresh leaves are added when needed.

Try This:

After establishing the worm farm, plant a few seeds in the container to create a miniature organic garden. The worms will aerate the soil and help the plants grow.

Butterfly Bottle

Nature Connection:

Butterflies and moths go through four stages of *metamorphosis* (change): 1) egg, 2) *larva* (caterpillar), 3) pupa (chrysalis—butterfly or cocoon—moth), and 4) adult. Children may watch the change from caterpillar to adult by constructing this butterfly bottle.

What You Need:

- clear, 2-liter plastic bottle, empty with wrapper removed
- caterpillar
- twigs and leaves from area where caterpillar was found
- sugar water (1½ teaspoons of sugar in 1 cup water)
- cotton ball
- soil
- clear plastic wrap
- butterfly identification guide
- spray bottle filled with water
- masking tape
- thick, strong rubber band
- scissors
- pencil

What You Do:

1. Have an adult cut off the neck and part of the top of the plastic bottle. Then, wrap masking tape around the sharp edges of the bottle. (You should be able to get your hand inside).
2. Put about an inch of soil at the bottom of the bottle. Stand some twigs up in the bottle. Add leaves and any materials that were found around the caterpillar. Place a caterpillar inside. Keep a fresh daily supply of leaves for the caterpillar to eat in the bottle.
3. Spread plastic wrap over the top and secure it with a rubber band. Poke several small holes in the plastic wrap with the point of a pencil. This is the lid.
4. Spray the inside of the bottle with water often enough to keep droplets on the leaves.
5. When the caterpillar has formed a cocoon or chrysalis, take out the leaves.
6. As the butterfly or moth emerges, spray the cage with water very well. The first thing the butterfly or moth will need is water.
7. The butterfly or moth will need food next. Moisten a cotton ball with sugar water and place the cotton ball in the bottle for food.
8. Observe the moth or butterfly for a day or two and then release it.

Try This:

Glue construction paper wings, wiggly eyes, and pipe cleaner antennae to a clothespin. This man-made butterfly can be displayed permanently in the Butterfly Bottle.

Colorful Sand Pictures

Nature Connection:

Natural sand is formed when rocks are ground down over time by wind or water. The fragments of rock are dragged along by the water or blown by the wind, then deposited on land to form a sandy beach.

Some artists use colored sand to create beautiful works of art. Children can do the same thing by coloring their own sand and gluing it onto tagboard.

What You Need:

- white sand
- tagboard
- powdered tempera paints (various colors)
- paper cups *or* small jars
- white glue
- plastic spoons
- pencil
- 1" paintbrush

What You Do:

1. Draw a simple design on the tagboard with a pencil.

2. Mix some sand with the tempera in a paper cup until the desired color is created. Prepare several colors in this way.

3. Look at the design and make a plan for where to place the colors.

4. Paint a light coating of glue on one section of the design. Cover the wet glue with one color of sand. Allow to dry completely. Shake off any excess sand.

5. Continue the process until you have covered all the sections of the design. Set the sand picture aside to dry.

Try This:

Use the newly-created colorful sand to make a sand jar. Use a funnel to pour each color of sand into a straight-edged jar (such as a baby food jar). Layer the colors in an alternating pattern. Fill the jar to the very top and use a tight seal, cap, or cork to hold the sand in place. Add a bow on top and give the sand jar to someone special.

Garden Caddy

Nature Connection:

Gardening is closely associated with the art and science of *horticulture*, a branch of agriculture that specializes in the growing of vegetables, flowers, fruits, trees, and shrubs. Like any scientist, a gardener requires tools, and, of course, a place to keep those tools! Have children construct this easy-to-carry tote to hold anything they may need to work in the garden.

What You Need:

- caddy patterns (page 52)
- 2 boxes of the same size (small cereal boxes work well)
- white adhesive-backed paper to cover both boxes
- permanent markers of various colors
- white glue
- scissors

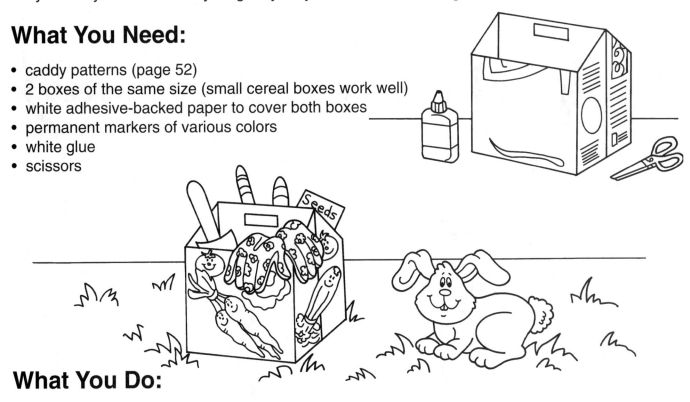

What You Do:

1. Have an adult cut both boxes according to the illustration shown above.
2. Glue the boxes firmly back to back. Allow to dry.
3. Cut a handle from the center section.
4. Cover the entire tote with adhesive-backed paper. The caddy should look the same from the front and back.
5. Draw colorful garden designs on the white background or copy, color, and cut out the caddy patterns to glue onto the Garden Caddy.

Try This:

Make this handy tote and fill it with seed packets, gloves, and a trowel for a useful and practical gift.

Summer

Garden Caddy

Garden Journal

Nature Connection:

Today, millions of people are considered to be home gardeners. Many children, as well, take pride in growing their own food. Have them use this Garden Journal to record observations made while learning how to plant, tend, and grow plants.

What You Need:

- Garden Journal cover pattern (page 54)
  or crayons, markers, and dried flowers
- Garden Journal sheet (page 55)
- strip of writing/drawing paper, 8" x 24" *or* 8" x 32"
- 2 pieces of tagboard, 8" squares
- 4 pieces of narrow ribbon *or* yarn, 24" length
- pencil
- scissors
- ruler
- white glue

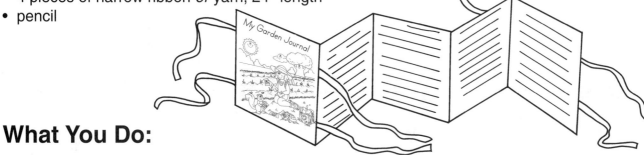

What You Do:

1. Fold the paper back and forth (accordion-style) until the book is a closed 8" square. You may need to measure off the first square to get the folded pages started correctly.

2. For the cover, copy the Garden Journal pattern, cut it out, and glue it to the tagboard. As an alternative, decorate a piece of tagboard using crayons, markers, and dried flowers. Then, print a title on the cover.

3. Glue two 24" lengths of ribbon across the front page, one toward the top, one toward the bottom of the page. (About 8" of ribbon should extend from each end.)

4. Repeat with the back page, gluing the other two lengths of ribbon across the page.

5. Glue the cover to the front of the journal on top of the ribbon. Glue the second piece of tagboard to the back of the journal on top of the ribbon. The ends of the ribbon will tie the finished book shut.

6. Copy and insert or glue the Garden Journal sheet inside the Garden Journal to help record observations of nature.

Try This:

Encourage children to set aside time each day during the gardening season to write in their journals. They can record observations, make predictions and drawings, or write original poetry and stories.

Garden Journal

Garden Journal

Garden Journal

1. What vegetables do you have in your garden?

_____

2. What flowers do you have in your garden?

_____

3. What kinds of birds have you seen?

_____

4. What kinds of bugs have you seen?

_____

5. What is you favorite item in the garden?

_____

6. What ways has the weather affected your garden?

_____

7. What do you like most about having a garden?

_____

Initial Garden

Nature Connection:

Radish seeds germinate quickly and mature in about four weeks. They will do best outdoors, but can be grown inside in a sunny window. Radishes do not require special fertilizers and will tolerate overwatering. Because the seeds are small and easy to manipulate, try planting them in creative ways. This craft explains how to grow radish sprouts in the shape of a letter or number.

What You Need:

- deep, clean, plastic tray (from a frozen dinner)
- radish seeds
- potting soil (enough to put 1½" layer in tray)
- water
- hand trowel

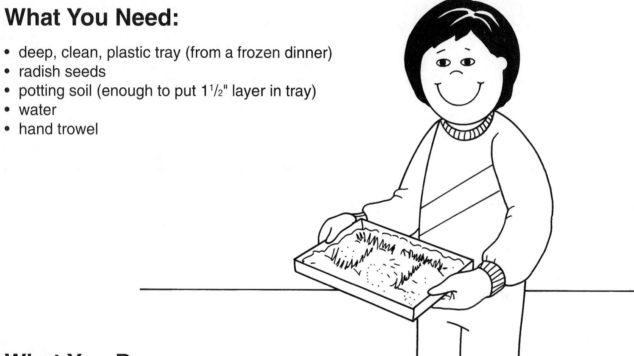

What You Do:

1. Put a 1½" layer of soil in the bottom of the plastic tray. Loosen and mix the soil with a trowel.
2. Decide on a letter or letters of the alphabet (possibly the child's initials) or a number, and outline those shapes in the soil with a finger.
3. Plant the radish seeds along the outline ½" deep and 2"–3" apart.
4. Water lightly. Sprouts should appear in about ten days. Do not allow the radishes to dry out completely.

Try This:

On a larger scale, spell out a whole word or name in a small plot of ground by using an entire crop of such things as carrots or beets.

Insect Magnets

Nature Connection:

The life cycle of most insects has four distinct stages: egg, larva, pupa, and adult. During each stage, insects experience a complete *metamorphosis* or "change in form." As students make these insect magnets, let them know that the ladybugs they are creating (on this page) are in the "adult" stage, and the caterpillars they are creating (on the next page) are in the "larva" stage.

What You Need:

- insect patterns (page 59)
- red and black felt squares (for ladybug magnet)
- green *or* brown felt squares (for caterpillar magnet)
- cardboard scraps
- magnetic tape (with peel-and-press backing)
- black, broad-point, felt-tipped marker
- 1–2 black pipe cleaners
- scissors
- white glue
- ruler

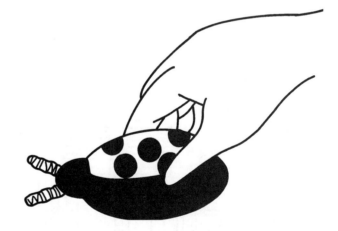

What You Do:

To Make a Ladybug Magnet:

1. Use the ladybug body pattern to cut a body shape from the cardboard and black felt.
2. Cut two 1" lengths of pipe cleaner.
3. Glue the pipe cleaners in place on the cardboard to make antennae.
4. Glue the black felt to the cardboard over the antennae.
5. Use the ladybug wing pattern to cut wings from the red felt.
6. Add black dots to the felt with a broad-point marker.
7. Glue the wings in place on top of the black felt body shape.
8. Cut a 1" piece of magnetic tape and secure it to the underside of the ladybug.

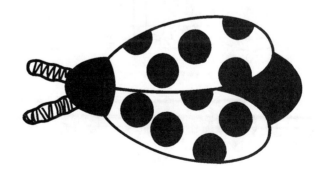

Insect Magnets

To Make a Caterpillar Magnet:

1. Cut a piece of cardboard using the caterpillar base pattern.
2. Cut two 1" lengths of pipe cleaner.
3. Glue in place on the cardboard to make antennae.
4. Use the caterpillar body pattern to cut five circles from the green or brown felt.
5. Use the marker to decorate one of the felt pieces for the caterpillar's face.
6. Glue the felt circles into place on the cardboard, overlapping slightly. Begin with the last body section and finish with the head.
7. Cut a 2" piece of magnetic tape and secure it to the underside of the caterpillar.

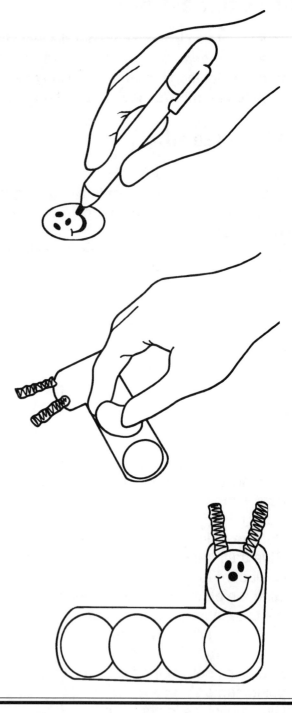

Try This:

These handmade insects can be turned into decorative pins. Just glue a pin latch to the back of the cardboard instead of magnetic tape. They make great gifts for a true "bug lover!"

Ladybug Magnet:

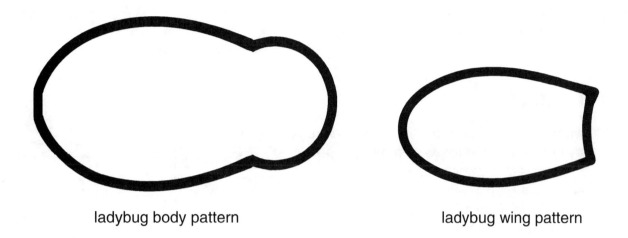

ladybug body pattern   ladybug wing pattern

Caterpillar Magnet:

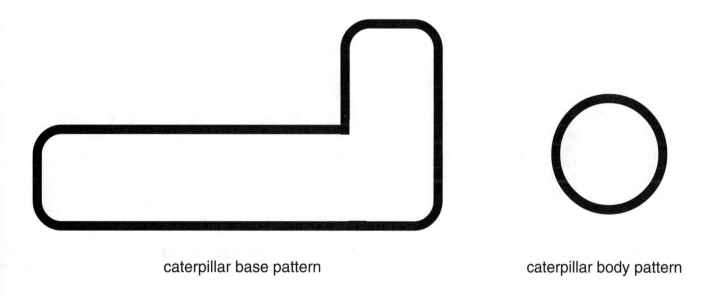

caterpillar base pattern   caterpillar body pattern

Summer

Pressed-Flower Sun Catcher

Nature Connection:

The sun is the center of our solar system, with the planets following individual orbits around it. The sun is one million times larger than the Earth, but it looks small because it is 93 million miles away. Providing energy for life on Earth, the sun generates heat and light. Children can capture the beauty of this light with a simple, floral sun catcher that can be hung in a window.

What You Need:

- pressed flowers (like pansies or daisies) and their leaves (If using heavier flowers, like roses, remove the petals and press them separately, then reassemble on the adhesive paper.)
- heavy book (or Flower Press from page 38)
- 2 pieces of clear, adhesive-backed paper, 8" square
- large, sturdy paper clip
- cord, 6" length
- scissors

What You Do:

1. Press flowers in the center of a book or flower press. Leave for 3-4 days.
2. Cut an 8" circle from each piece of adhesive paper.
3. Peel the backing from one circle of adhesive paper.
4. On the sticky side of the paper, arrange the flowers in the center. Press to hold them in place.
5. For hanging, place a large paper clip on one edge, so that about half of the paper clip is pressed onto the paper.
6. Peel the backing from the other circle of adhesive paper. Carefully place it on top of the flowers and press to seal the pieces of adhesive paper together. Trim any edges that do not overlap.
7. Hang the sun catcher in a window, so that it will catch and reflect the light.

Try This:

Make a colorful book cover for a book about flowers. Complete the sun catcher as a square but do not include the paper clip. Staple it to the front of collected drawings of flowers.

Quick-and-Easy Sundial

Nature Connection:

Shadows are caused as the sun moves across the sky. Many years ago, people used shadows cast by sundials to tell time. Children can use these same principles to construct their own sundials. Keep in mind, that the stick in a true sundial would be angled perfectly according to the latitude of the city in which the sundial rests. For the demonstration purposes of this craft, however, it is sufficient simply to angle the stick toward the north.

What You Need:

- yellow tagboard circle, 12" diameter
  or white tagboard circle, 12" diameter, with yellow marker
- new pencil *or* 10" dowel
- medium-sized rock (optional)
- ruler
- black marker
- scissors
- white glue
- small hammer
- compass
- sunny day

What You Do:

1. If using white tagboard, color the tagboard circle with a yellow marker.
2. Use the ruler to mark the center of the circle and make a small hole with scissors.
3. Go outside on a sunny day, and use the compass to find north.
4. Push the pencil or dowel through the center of the circle, and tap it into the ground. Angle the pencil or dowel toward the north.
5. Label the hour at the point where the shadow reaches the edge of the circle.
6. If it is a windy day, place a rock on the sundial to keep it from spinning.
7. Go back to the sundial every hour and mark the movement of the shadow around the edge of the circle with the corresponding hour.

Try This:

Find a friend and make a human sundial. On a sunny day, draw a large circle on the playground with chalk and mark an X in the exact center. Stand on the X, then have your friend make a mark at the end of your shadow and label with the time every hour.

Summer Bird Feeder

Nature Connection:

Most birds are helpful to gardeners because they eat the insects, caterpillars, and slugs that harm crops. At a glance, most birds can be identified as seed-eaters or insect-eaters. Seed-eaters have short, small bills that they use for crunching seeds. Insect-eaters have long, narrow bills that they use to reach into holes and pluck out unsuspecting bugs. It is easy for children to provide food for seed-eating birds in this easy-to-make bird feeder.

What You Need:

- hollowed-out $\frac{1}{2}$ fruit shell (orange or grapefruit works best)
- scissors
- string, four 1" lengths
- bird seed
- bird food, such as bread, dry corn, cranberries, popcorn, etc.

What You Do:

1. With scissors, poke four small holes at equal distances in the top edge of a hollowed-out $\frac{1}{2}$ fruit shell. (Save the left over fruit for the Try This activity below.)

2. Tie a length of string from each hole. Gather the four strings at the top and tie them together into a sturdy knot.

3. Fill the shell with bird seed and bird food.

4. Hang the feeder from a tree branch. Extra string may be needed to tie the feeder to a thick branch.

5. Watch the birds flock to the feeder!

Try This:

Another type of bird feeder can be made with a mesh bag used to store onions or oranges. Fill the bag with large pieces of bird food, such as stale bread slices, pieces of fruit, and chunks of suet. Tie the bag closed with a length of string and hang it from a tree branch.

Window Box Garden

Nature Connection:

A window box can be a manageable garden for young children. Its long, narrow shape and portability make planting convenient. An adult should guide children when selecting and arranging their plants, however, so that they consider a plant's size when fully grown. Children should also remember to include some trailing plants and others with decorative leaves to give variety to their window garden. A garden placed in a sunny window will provide a colorful display for many weeks.

What You Need:

- window box patterns (page 64)
- shoe box with lid
- crayons and markers
- several small bedding plants (petunias, impatiens, geraniums, pansies, marguerite, vinca vines, etc.)
- small plastic bag (wastebasket size–13 gallon)
- potting soil
- gravel
- water
- liquid fertilizer
- hand trowel

What You Do:

1. Decorate the shoe box with crayons and markers or copy, color, and cut out the window box patterns to glue onto the box.

2. Line the shoe box with the small plastic bag and set the upturned lid underneath the box for durability.

3. Put about 1" of gravel in the bottom.

4. Fill the box half full of potting soil.

5. Experiment with several different plant arrangements. Tall plants should be in the back, vining ones in the front. When the best arrangement has been chosen, carefully remove the plants from their pots and put them in place on the soil. Fill in around the plants with enough soil to hold them firmly.

6. Set the box in a sunny window.

7. Water the plants. Check the water every 2–3 days. Keep the plants moist. Remove dead flower heads every day.

8. To have the best flower production, apply liquid fertilizer to the window box every six weeks.

Try This:

Use the window box garden to grow an "edible treat" by planting vegetable seeds such as radishes or tomatoes.

Summer

Window Box